yellow roses

robert l. o'keefe

Cover design by Aaron M. O'Keefe

Yellow Roses

ISBN: 979-8-218-73585-2

Skinsuit Communciations First Edition
Skinsuit@SKsuit.com

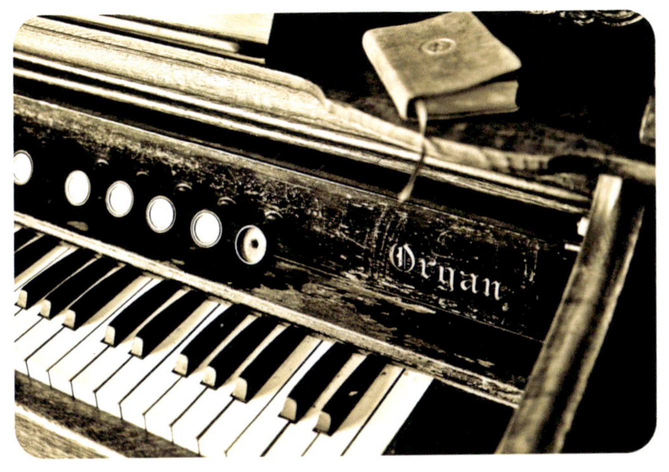

Robert L. O'Keefe
5/22/1949 - 1/18/2019

loved & missed

Foreword

Conceived to be a collaborative project between father and son fifteen years ago, *Yellow Roses* is a collection of poems by Robert L. O'Keefe paired with select photographic work of mine. This collection of my father's work touches on a wide range of topics that are thematic across the span of his work. While themes of over-development, the loss of childhood innocence, and Native American history were all consistent in his work, the most personal and emotionally powerful selections are exemplfied in the book's title piece, "Yellow Roses."

My father held all of his children and grandchildren as the most important part of his life. In our conversations revolving around this project, when it was just an inkling of an idea, he and I spoke of it as a sort of healing process for him, as he was trying to come to terms with the loss of one of his daughters, Colleen O'Keefe Craig. Yellow Roses is, in my mind, a doorway into my dad's journey to make sense of it all.

As time passed, this project was shelved because "life happens" and we all fall victim to the distractions of day-to-day life. What originally began as a collaborative effort between my dad and me has now evolved into something much larger and personal to me. Robert L. O'Keefe, my father, passed away on January 18th, 2019. It's funny how life is very cyclical and how this project quickly became for me what it was to him, a way for me to make sense of his loss and a journey to heal so that I can be the best father, uncle, son, and friend to those I hold dear to me.

This project has been a very arduous and emotional journey for me. It has also been fulfilling and beautiful as well. So I repeat myself... What was originally meant to be a simple collaboration between a father and son has become a much more grand journey that culminates in me being able to honor my father and the memories he left us with. May this book and the artistic works inspired by my father's words be a testament to the incredibly large and inclusive heart that he had.

May all who had the chance to know my dad find as much joy in reading his words as I do.

-Aaron M. O'Keefe

Table of Contents

Identify 1
Custer 2
Forever? 3
Non Sequitur 5
Painless 6
Money Don't Rhyme with Funny 7
Absolute Immorality 9
Retrospect 11
Completely Clueless 12
Stranded 13
Ides 14
Futurama 16
Last Gasp 17
Hysterical Accuracy 19
Osama Bin Token 21
The Holiday Feast 23
In the Saddle Too Long 24
Thus Spoke Sarathustra/ Misconceptions Revisited 25
Babylon 27
House of the Rove Inn Sun 28
Nothing Sacred 30
POV 31
Goal Oriented 32
#23 34
Pagan Ritual 36
A Crazy Shade of Winter 37
Code of Conduct 39
Showdown at the Gateway 41
Yellow Roses 43

IDENTIFY

conflict
armed or unarmed
has historical consistency
motivated by short term urgency
from biblical to current
we find no lasting deterrent
a rise in the seven deadly sins
usually at the core of how it begins
noble causes may be spoke
but always beneath a darker cloak
some insidiously murky rationale
results in a massive fatale
the unyielding enemy
in the mirror we see.

CUSTER

is it going badly
this western war we find
it began so easily
now there's no end to it
more and more casualties daily
with little to show for the price
even the general public
has begun to grumble
for the other side
now there's a large force massing
for a full scale attack
we need a reckless hero
some valiant popular rascal
where's Pickett when we need him
to mount a heroic charge
against an ominous enemy
win or lose
we win.

FOREVER?

what purpose
does this quest serve
easily the life cut short
leaves potential for tragedy
but to what purpose
this last one standing venue
                                        the machismo
                                        of the old west gunfight
                                        enduring power
                                        of an elder statesman
                                        the futile quest
                                        of a long distance runner
a part time job
a vehicle
the middle stuff
between start and end
a sojourn
not a destination
an episode
but not the novel.

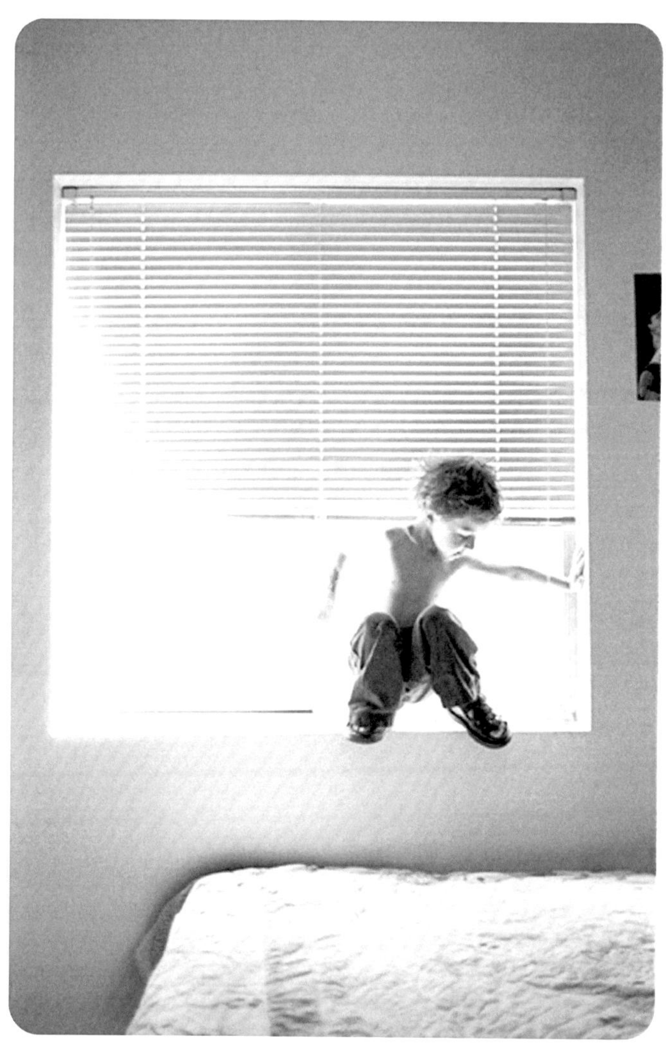

"The Window" *©2002 Aaron M. O'Keefe*

a pillar of civilization
the zenith of technology
a lighthouse for the oppressed
the premier food grower to the world
the healthcare care and research nirvana
the example of opportunity and ingenuity
the entertainment and amusement kingfish
the most desirable lifestyle
a cultural haven for the arts
                    the most powerful arsenal
                    and the leading adolescent suicide rate

Non sequitur

PAINLESS

how long this baggage
has been on the train
it has been an arduous trek
and the baggage does pile up
young lives lost
young loves lost
senseless tragedies
old friends drifting away
a serpentine journey
endless dramas of all sorts
the endless rattle and hum
as life's locomotive
pours down the double rails
always a new adventure ahead
always more baggage for the baggage car
a constant tug-of-war
between new discoveries
and fading memoirs
an emotional juggernaut
with only one stop
and no transfers.

MONEY DON'T RHYME WITH FUNNY

idealism can be tricky
perspective being enigmatic
and the topics prophetic
everything from Valhalla to Sara Lee
but this is no crumb cake

a lifestyle revisited
a simplistic system revisited
let's eliminate the directive
and retool the perspective
into a someplace that could be anywhere

first we gotta eat
etch providers names in the dirt
even give them a special shirt
to them to deliver red meat
then we gotta stay dry
so another group maintains the camp
so no bones suffer from the damp
and all have a warm dry place to lie
then comes the caregivers
warm words for sagging hearts
thick hides for cold body parts
then comes the dreamers
to counsel the young
to rekindle the not so young
verbal streamers carrying the traditions

but but but
the do-gooders interrupt
with the brash tirade
where are the politicians
where are the 7-11s
where are the high-rises
where are the stores
where are the cell phones
where’s the paycheck

grand thoughts and idyllic dreams
lost on simple simons
for if it don’t make money
it ain’t squat
even though it had lasted generations

ABSOLUTE IMMORALITY

when people are living
in cardboard boxes
when healthcare
is for a chosen few
when food pantries
are running on empty
when school funding
has no priority
when crisis intervention centers
get high-school allowances

$600 a plate fund raisers.

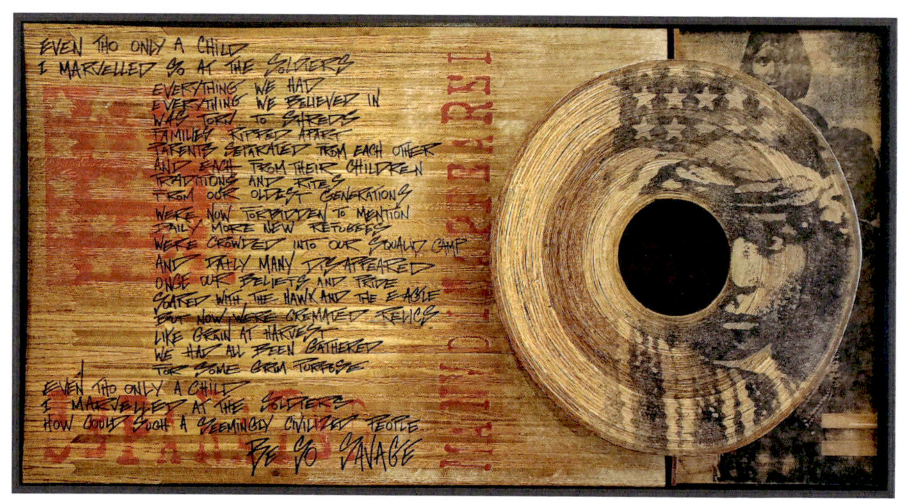

"Memoirs of a Holocaust" *©2020 Aaron M. O'Keefe*

RETROSPECT

I can cover my ears
to block out the traffic, horns
trains, planes, and big rigs
to hear again the songbirds
and the whisper of the wind
          I can cover my eyes
          to block out the high-rises,
          highways, malls, and sub-divisions
          to again see oceans of tall grasses
          and clear unbordered horizons
I can cover my mouth
to cover the inane daily banter
to speak of the old ways
of traditional rituals and values
          I can cover my mind
          to block out the indulgent waste
          to times when all had value
          everything shared and nothing wasted
but I cannot cover my heart
it has no such boundary
and still bleeds for Wounded Knee.

COMPLETELY CLUELESS

from the dusky hill
outside Jerusalem where
a prophet died
                    from the great American west
                    where an entire nation of people
                    were systematically erased
from the New Mexico desert
where all existing life-forms
were robbed of innocence by a mushroom cloud
                    from a Dallas motorcade
                    where an entire generation
                    was shot in the conscience
from the Memphis hotel walkway
the sins of generations were
expunged by an assassin
                    from a California hotel back hallway
                    where a new generation's dreams
                    ran red on the floor
from the hilly outskirts of Bethlehem
where riot police and armored cars
have replaced shepherds at the stable.

STRANDED

first strike
as old as turn the other cheek
a preventative action for the meek
or a more civilized path to seek

after singular events
easy rationale for building a fence
not seemingly overreactive
but in reality who's the captive

reaction to a perceived threat
may not be a safe bet
for if we turn back the historical tick tock
the natives would've left us on Plymouth Rock.

IDES

O Jericho
hub of civilization
center of learning
walled city of power
cultural gathering place
indomitable fortress
shining city on the hill
        fear not the lone figure
        on the distant hill
        tis only Joshua
        and history awaits you.

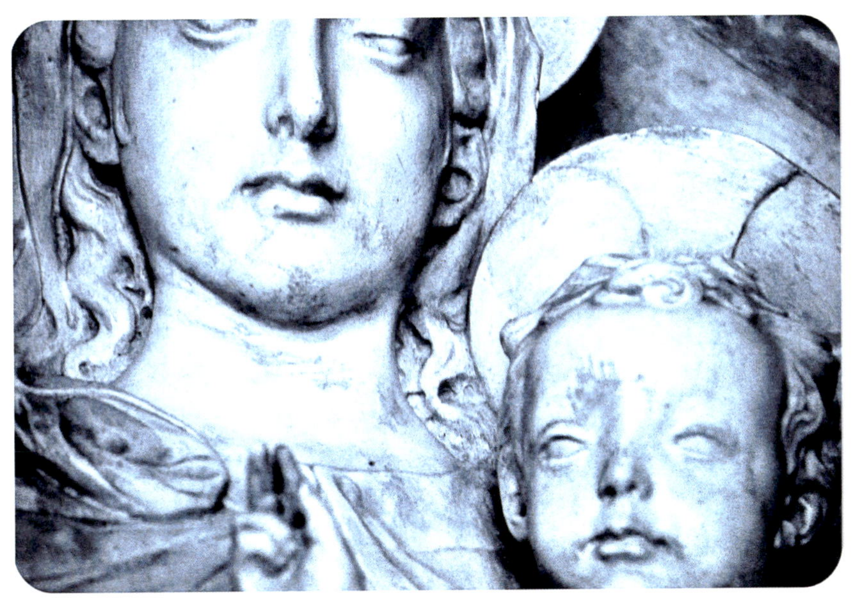

"Mother & Child" ©2011 *Aaron M. O'Keefe*

FUTURAMA

yesterday
wrought with if's
laced with life's petty tiffs
awash with emotional lifts
a myriad of paths taken
and of causes forsaken
and signals mistaken

history
serves no ethic
simple record of events
fodder for the learning machine

yesterday
is what it was
the day before
very much like it
only tomorrow
is yet to be written.

LAST GASP

a cyclical journey
from first breath
to inevitable end
sometimes on slo-mo
sometimes on fast forward
sometimes on play
but never on rewind
always on
oft lost and forgotten
in daily pursuits and distractions
an impassionate partner
in everything we do.

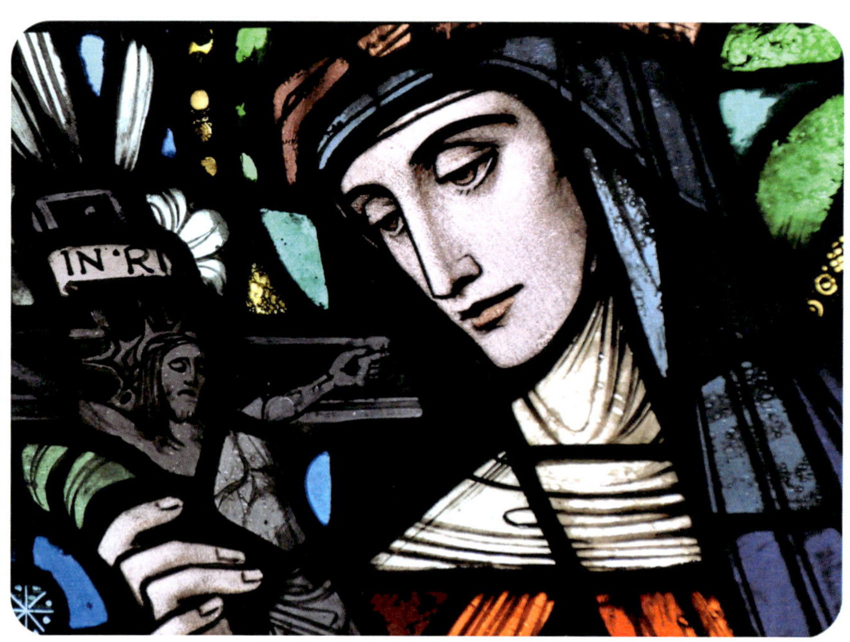

"Saint Malo's Glass" *©2012 Aaron M. O'Keefe*

HYSTERICAL ACCURACY

something new
something different
just a new name
but it's really the same
left to itself
history has no ulterior plot
for we are but a simple lot
one dimensionally thou shalt not
    but somehow when max factoring the facts
    to rationalize our acts
    by liberally spreading the mascara
    we sound as logical as Yogi Berra
never afraid of an oxymoron
actually never beyond a regular moron
we are off on a holy war
translation: someone's coming home on a door
    but when it's turned on us
    you might as well just start up the bus
    unbelievable the squalling fuss
    when the ethic turns on us
in the same breath as Nazi
never mention Wounded Knee
    you thought they cringed at McCarthy's file
    just mention the holy Roman pedophile
when the armored tanks visit Bethlehem's stable
was it merely a perversion of Aesop's Fable
    Pearl Harbor was as bitter as sake
    so we countered with Nagasaki

we could plead insanity at Heaven's gate
but that's all water under the gate
                    civilizing the jungles of Borneo
                    with our colonoscopy video
making a million-dollar bomb smart
but no cash for little Johnny's art
                    raucously cheering Louise and Thelma
                    too bad they all couldn't catch the bus to Selma
a shining society with nothing to hyde
except for adolescent suicide
                    history has its prognostication
                    no eternal civilization.

OSAMA BIN TOKEN

an ailing icon
a target
in a limited range
an exile
with a bounty
should stand out
like Santa Claus in Kenya
why no success
with all the technology
with all the horsepower
amassed in the hunt
but then
how do you cry wolf
with no wolf.

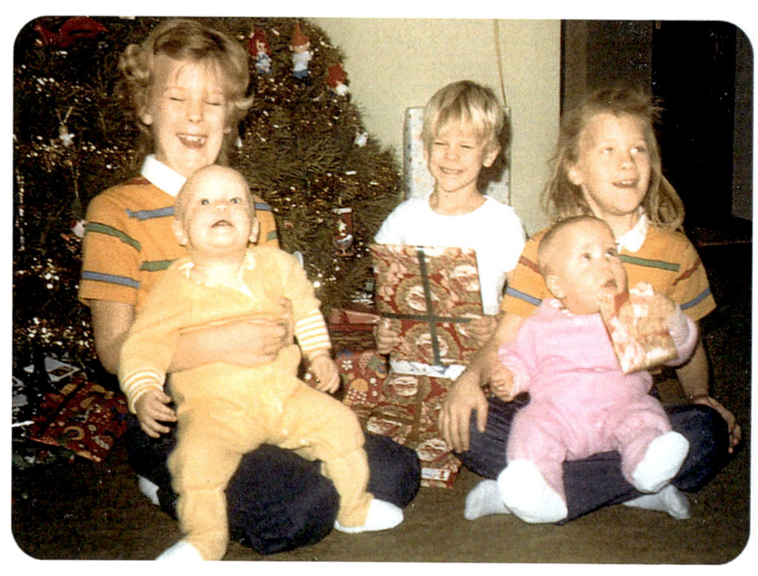

Family photo December 1980

THE HOLIDAY FEAST

the large stately tables
adorned with decorative finery
covered with culinary delights
and heavenly scents fill the air
gifts surround a festive tree
and the little ones giggle constantly
and yet there is a somber side
                    concerning those empty chairs
and Scrooge's ghosts
visions of feasts gone by
past us swiftly fly
but the focus of the feast
is not the empty chairs there
rather those that are full.

IN THE SADDLE TOO LONG

when was the last time
you sat outside late at night
just to count the stars
        when was the last time
        you gazed into a child's eyes
        to see the love and faith there
when was the last time
a sorrow cut your heart so deep
that you felt you could bleed no more
        when was the last time
        you let a teardrop crawl
        all the way down your cheek
when was the last time
you held someone's hand
and really felt their heartbeat
        when was the last time
        you let another creature fall asleep in your arms
        and learned what trust was all about
when was the last time
you got off life's merry-go-round
to wonder why it's a circle
        if you can't remember
        you've been on the freeway too long.

THUS SPOKE SARATHUSTRA / MISCONCEPTIONS REVISITED

ask and you shall receive
    who would ever be disappointed
    we rarely know what we want or want what we know

Cinderella and Prince Charming
    Madison Avenue lies
    ogres, trolls, and fairies need love too

it's supposed to be fair out there
    it ain't . . . wear a cup

if you play by the rules nothing bad will happen
    fortunately we don't control the strings . . . ship happens

truth in advertising
    if it's that great why do you have to try so hard to sell it

sooner or later it gets easier
    gradually we eliminate repeat errors but ship still happens

bad people will never succeed
    religious voodoo . . . even bathtub scum rises to the top

seek and you will find
    life is beautiful . . . it won't come to you . . . ya gotta go find it

rebates, coupons, cuts in line, discounts, seniority, priority seating
    null and void at the pearly gates
    . . . might want to get used to the idea early.

"God Demands It" *©2008 Aaron M. O'Keefe*

BABYLON

for all the power
for all the glory
where are Babylon
and Jericho now
beyond the fortresses
beyond the walls
beyond the palaces
for all the power
for all the glory
where are carthage
and the mongul horde now
beyond the culture
beyond the conquests
for all the power
for all the glory
where are the mings
and the Aztecs now
history
the impartial ultimate tutor
for our arrogant stupor.

HOUSE OF THE ROVE INN SUN

there is a house
in Washington
they call the Rove Inn Sun
and it's been the ruin
of many a poor boy
and God, I know, I'm one

my mother was a Bircher
so I seemed to fit right in
my father was an ex-GI
so I knew not to ask them why

now the only thing a Rove Inn knows
is to twist and tangle words
and the only time he is satisfied
is when he's polishing turds

o mothers
tell your children
not to do what I have done
spend their life in pure skullduggery
in the house of the Rove Inn Sun

the Inn it has no back door
so I must finish the game
I'm going back to Washington
to the bull shovelers hall of fame.

Apologies to Eric Burdon and the Animals

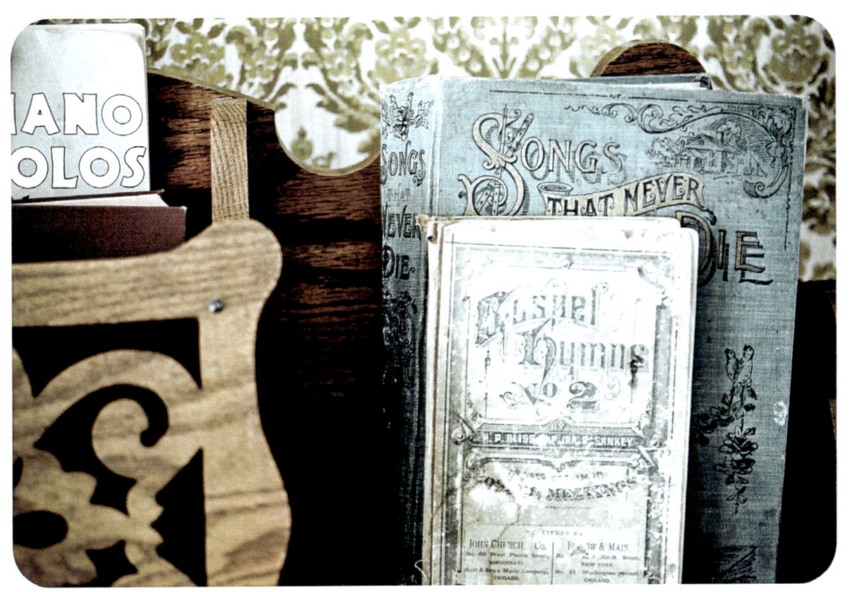

"Songs That Never Die" *©2014 Aaron M. O'Keefe*

NOTHING SACRED

dinner
not a 14-course buffet

shelter
not a 12-room gated estate

career
not stock options and six-figure bonuses

husbands
not Cialis junkies

wives
not Maybelline Stepfords

protection
not 22-round semi-automatic clips

worship
not 17-cable channel evangelism

beverage
not a 64-ounce Big Gulp

pride
not just always #1

politics
not just big brother in gift-wrap

enlightenment
not just programmed educational degrees.

POV

huddled amidst the hanging winter coats
thru the crack in the door
from my embryonic haven
I can smell the pine
wafting through the moth-balled closet air
and a fire of sorts
hearing its random crackle and snap
    and crisp cedar burnt scent
    carefully peeking
    neither seen nor heard
    I envision the sight
    a wondrously decorated X-mas tree
    and a raging hearth
    but from where I sit
    it could be a campfire
    and a whole forest of trees
    so much lost
    to unopened doors.

GOAL ORIENTED

are you going
to the park today
to watch the trees
cast their cooling shadows
to maybe push a swing
for a little one in need
to sit and really listen
to the birds joyous song
to gaze the clouds pathway
across a deep blue sky
to smell the fresh cut grass
and the flowers sweet incense
to hear the unbridled laughter
of the children at play
are you going
to the park today.

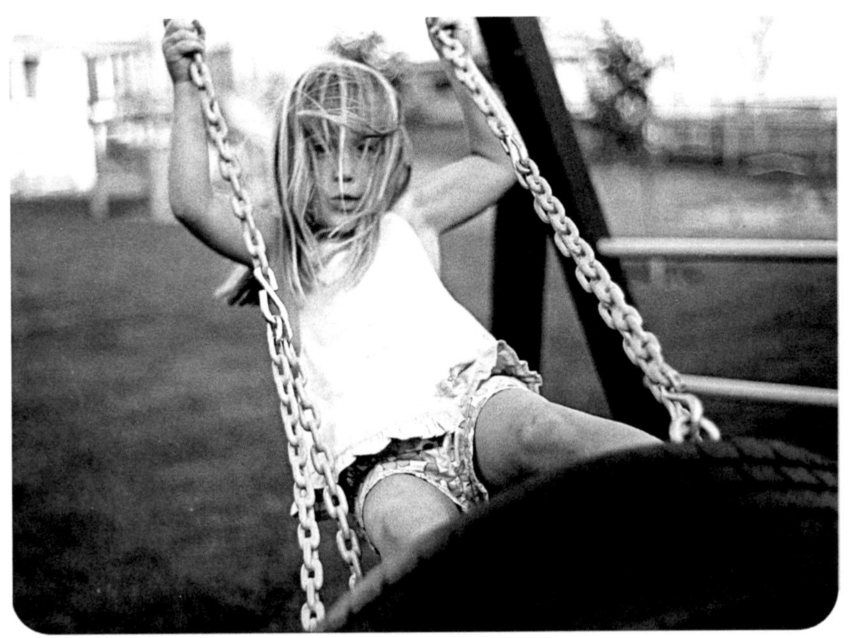

"The Swing" *©2002 Aaron M. O'Keefe*

#23

this tree
has many callings to see
several generations of memories growing upwardly
has left a virtual myriad of visions before me
    a nest for birds singing gleefully
    a giant shadow coolly cast
    a vault for nuts squirreled safely
    a generous umbrella against a raindrop fest
    a glue for soil held securely
    a midnight shadow cast eerily
    or carved initials held tenderly
what fate awaits the tree
carefully numbered #23
sadly it's where the new driveway will be.

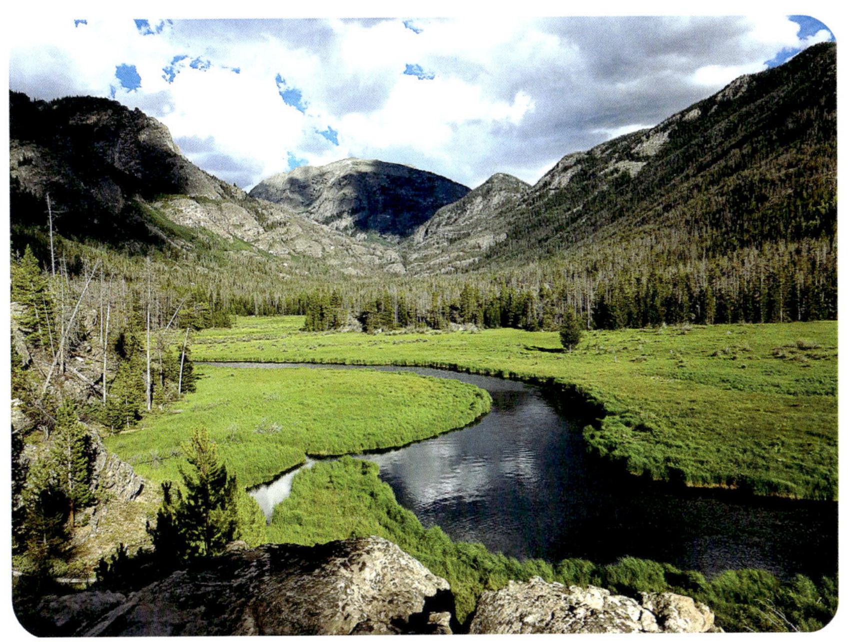

"Adams Falls Trailhead" *©2017 Aaron M. O'Keefe*

PAGAN RITUAL

do we rob
a robber

do we embezzle
an embezzler

do we beat
an abuser

do we steal
from a thief

do we burn
an arsonist

why is there
such a thrill
to drop the trap
throw the switch
inject the dose
why is the taste of blood
so sweet.

A CRAZY SHADE OF WINTER

to the mind's eye
just an early summer's day
lost in mid-November
blue sky and warm sun
radiating on the nearby barren trees
yielding to nature's course
this year's leaves have packed their bags
an endlessly predictable cycle of change
                    yet in the soul's eye
                    a melancholy tear forms
remembering spring capricious dance
an unbridled exuberance in youth
                    the frenzied roller-coaster of summer
                    a romping carnival adventure
the savory melancholy of fall
as a year passes towards spring's rebirth
                    the restless certainty of winter
                    a stark passage into reality
                    where the seasons colorful adventures
                    are cast against a barren backdrop
or are they all illusory
like so many seasonings in an old recipe.

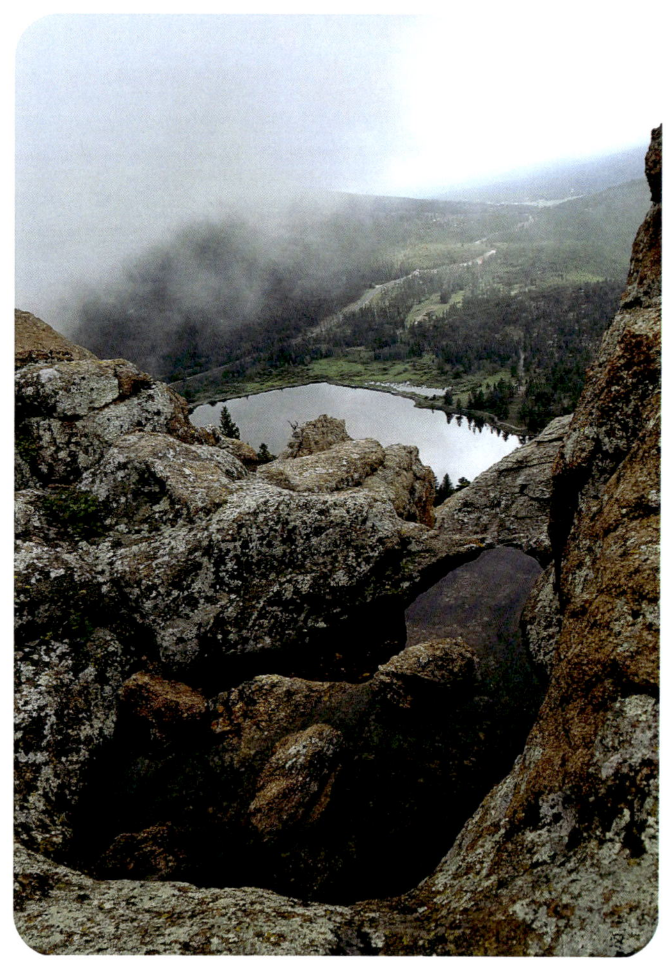

"The Edge of Time" *©2017 Aaron M. O'Keefe*

CODE OF CONDUCT

manifest destiny
gave this country a cause
and bared also some basic flaws

self-anointed crusaders
in gowns of saintly white
burning crosses at midnight

noble defenders of the free
to the ends of the Earth for liberation
but balking to this day with emancipation

a benevolent big brother
seeking worldwide to liberate
but still dragging our heels to integrate

acolytes of a tower of hope
policing the world against genocide
while the hometown favorite is suicide

caretakers of a shiny city
worldwide campaigning for democracy
but the ultimate truth is buried at Wounded Knee.

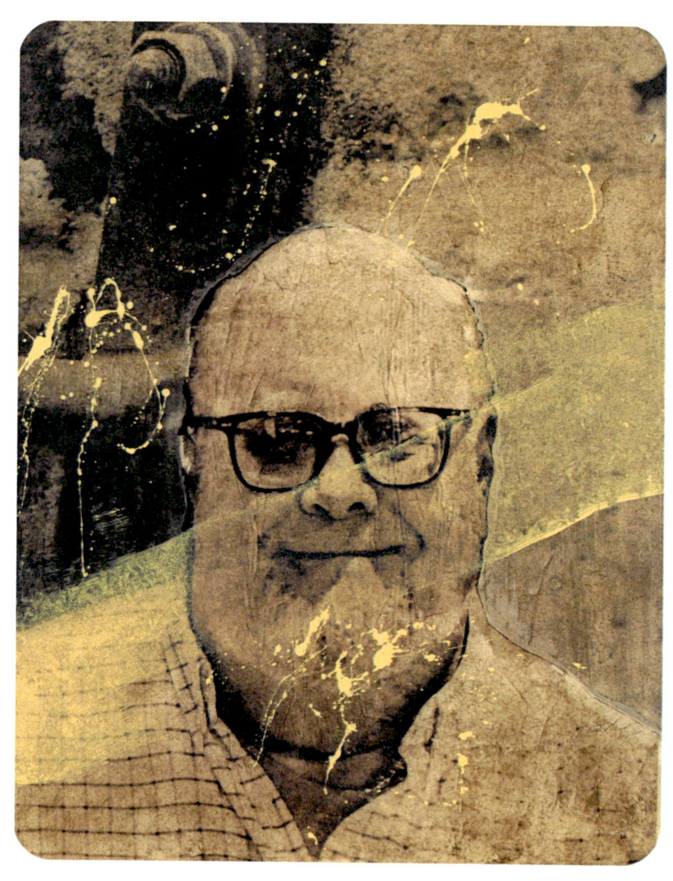

"A Heart I Still Long to Touch" *©2020 Aaron M. O'Keefe*

SHOWDOWN AT THE GATEWAY

not on tiptoes
with so much accumulated anxiety
not backwards
with cowering indecision
not sideways
with accidental discovery

but head-on
blow through the doors
like a gunfighter
into an old west saloon
daring to make an entrance
oblivious to the unknown

only a tragedy
for the unprepared.

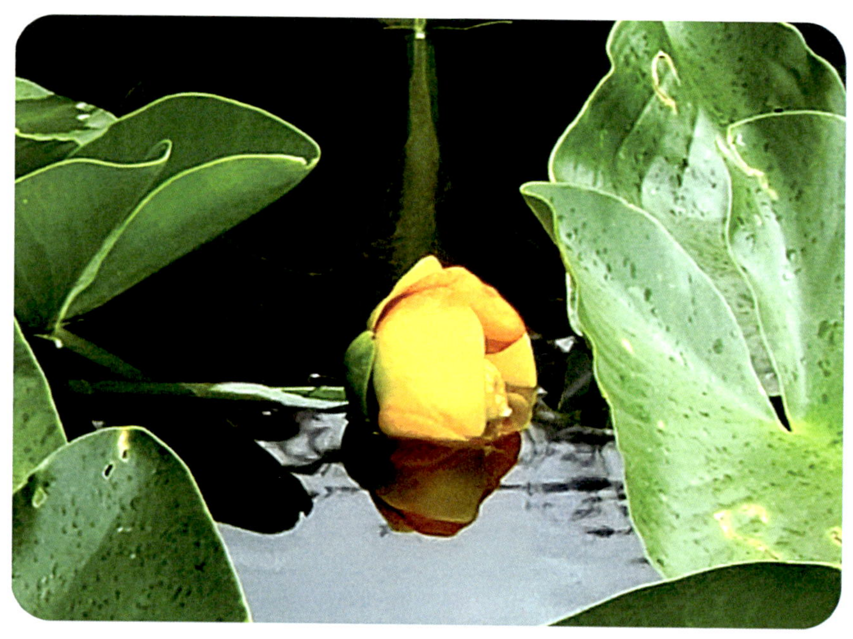

"Cub Lake" *©2019 Aaron M. O'Keefe*

YELLOW ROSES

1 1/2 years
    since I've heard that raucous laugh

18 months
    of fast-forward memories

76 weeks
    of dodging late Sunday afternoon phone calls

548 days
    waiting for a 3 p.m. phone call

13,152 hours
    searching for that Cheshire grin

789,120 minutes
    with an angel's hand on my shoulder
    like yesterday and forever together
    but who's counting.

Acknowledgements

This project would not be possible if it weren't for the love and support shown to me by countless loved ones in the days, weeks, months, etc. following the passing of my father. Without your kindness and compassion, none of this would have been possible. I am forever indebted to you. You have no idea what this has meant to me.

I would like to acknowledge two people specifically without whom this book would not have been possible. C. Daniel Newberry has been an incredible friend, mentor, and inspiration to me over the years. In my dad's absence, Dan has been by my side, offering support, guidance, wisdom, and kindness above all else. Dan has helped fill a void left by the passing of my father. I am forever thankful for everything you have done for me, Dan. Thank you.

I would also like to send out a sincere thank you to Rebecca Markus. Being an author herself, Rebecca possesses a deep knowledge of self publishing and all the steps involved in the process. Knowing how important this project is to me, Rebecca selflessly volunteered her time and her knowledge to help bring this project to life. I cannot express how thankful I am to Rebecca for her efforts. Thank you.

Lastly, I would like to thank everyone that was a part of my dad's life. Whether you were merely an acquaintance or a close friend, thank you for being a part of it. Because of your friendships, my dad lived a full life of joy and happiness. I know that he loved each and every one of you.

-Aaron M. O'Keefe

www.ingramcontent.com/pod-product-compliance
Ingram Content Group UK Ltd.
Pitfield, Milton Keynes, MK11 3LW, UK
UKRC032148290726
14090UKWH00012B/498